A CINEMATIC HISTORY of ACTION & ADVENTURE

www.raintreepublishers.co.uk
Visit our website to find out more information about Raintree books.

To order:
☎ Phone 44 (0) 1865 888113
📠 Send a fax to 44 (0) 1865 314091
💻 Visit the Raintree bookshop at www.raintreepublishers.co.uk to browse our catalogue and order online.

A CINEMATIC HISTORY OF ACTION & ADVENTURE was produced by

David West 🏃 Children's Books
7 Princeton Court
55 Felsham Road
London SW15 1AZ

Designer: Rob Shone
Editor: Rowan Lawton
Picture Research: Gail Bushnell

First published in Great Britain by
Raintree, Halley Court, Jordan Hill, Oxford OX2 8EJ, part of Harcourt Education. Raintree is a registered trademark of Harcourt Education Ltd.

Copyright © 2005 David West Children's Books

08 07 06 05
10 9 8 7 6 5 4 3 2 1

ISBN 1 844 21080 4

British Library Cataloguing in Publication Data

Wilshin, Mark
A cinematic history of action and adventure
1.Adventure films - History and criticism - Juvenile literature
I.Title
791.4'3655

Printed and bound in China

PHOTO CREDITS :
Abbreviations: t-top, m-middle, b-bottom, r-right, l-left, c-centre.

3, LUCASFILM LTD/PARAMOUNT / THE KOBAL COLLECTION; 4l, Photo By SNAP / REX FEATURES; 4r, WARNER BROS / THE KOBAL COLLECTION / COOPER, ANDREW; 5r WARNER BROS / THE KOBAL COLLECTION / COOPER, ANDREW; 6b, Photo By EVERETT COLLECTION / REX FEATURES; 6m, THE KOBAL COLLECTION / EDISON; 7t, LASKY PRODUCTIONS / THE KOBAL COLLECTION; 7bl, UNITED ARTISTS / THE KOBAL COLLECTION; 7br, Photo By EVERETT COLLECTION / REX FEATURES; 8l, Photo By REX FEATURES; 8r, Photo By C.MGM/EVERETT / REX FEATURES; 9t, WARNER BROS / THE KOBAL COLLECTION; 9m, Photo By SNAP / REX FEATURES; 9b, UNITED ARTISTS / THE KOBAL COLLECTION; 10t, Photo By SNAP / REX FEATURES; 10m, MGM / THE KOBAL COLLECTION; 11t, WARNER BROS / THE KOBAL COLLECTION; 11m, Photo By C.WARNER BR/EVERETT / REX FEATURES; 10b, Photo By C.20THC.FOX/EVERETT / REX FEATURES; 12l, Photo By EVERETT COLLECTION / REX FEATURES; 12r, 20TH CENTURY FOX / THE KOBAL COLLECTION; 13tl, Photo By C.COLUMBIA/EVERETT / REX FEATURES; 13tr, HERZOG/FILMVERLAG DER AUTOREN/ZDF / THE KOBAL COLLECTION; 13br, HERZOG/FILMVERLAG DER AUTOREN/ZDF / THE KOBAL COLLECTION; 13bl, WARNER BROS / THE KOBAL COLLECTION; 14t, Photo By C.20THC.FOX/EVERETT / REX FEATURES; 14b, Photo By C.20THC.FOX/EVERETT / REX FEATURES; 14/15t, Photo By C.W. DISNEY/EVERETT / REX FEATURES; 14/15m, Photo By EVERETT COLLECTION / REX FEATURES; 15l, Photo By C.20THC.FOX/EVERETT / REX FEATURES; 16t, DISNEY/RKO / THE KOBAL COLLECTION; 16b, Photo By SNAP / REX FEATURES; 17t, PARAMOUNT / THE KOBAL COLLECTION; 17m, LUCASFILM LTD/PARAMOUNT / THE KOBAL COLLECTION; 17b, THE KOBAL COLLECTION / LUCASFILM LTD/PARAMOUNT; 18l, Photo By EVERETT COLLECTION / REX FEATURES; 18r, UNITED ARTISTS / THE KOBAL COLLECTION; 18/19m, DANJAQ/EON/UA / THE KOBAL COLLECTION; 19t, Photo By EVERETT COLLECTION / REX FEATURES; 19m, DANJAQ/EON/UA / THE KOBAL COLLECTION; 19b, Photo By EVERETT COLLECTION / REX FEATURES; 20t, THE KOBAL COLLECTION / UFA; 20m, PARAMOUNT / THE KOBAL COLLECTION; 20b, MGM / THE KOBAL COLLECTION; 21t, UNITED ARTISTS / THE KOBAL COLLECTION / CAMBOULIVE, PATRICK; 21m, Photo By Robert Judges / Rex Features; 21b, PARAMOUNT / THE KOBAL COLLECTION; 22t, TOUCHSTONE / THE KOBAL COLLECTION / CHEN, LINDA R; 22b, Photo By EVERETT COLLECTION / REX FEATURES; 23t, Photo By EVERETT COLLECTION / REX FEATURES; 23m, Photo By SNAP / REX FEATURES; 23b, Photo By C.PARAMOUNT/EVERETT / REX FEATURES; 24t, NEW LINE/ROGER BIRNBAUM / THE KOBAL COLLECTION / MARSHAK, BOB; 24b, CONCORD/WARNER BROS / THE KOBAL COLLECTION; 24/25m, THE KOBAL COLLECTION / XIAN FILM STUDIO / ADYANI, SAEED; 25t, WARNER BROS / THE KOBAL COLLECTION / HILL, KHAREN; 25m, MGM/LAKESHORE/MOSAIC / THE KOBAL COLLECTION / KRAYCHYK, GEORGE; 25b, 20TH CENTURY FOX / THE KOBAL COLLECTION; 26t, Photo By SNAP / REX FEATURES; 26b,WARNER BROS / THE KOBAL COLLECTION; 27t, PARAMOUNT / MALPASO / THE KOBAL COLLECTION; 27m, 20TH CENTURY FOX / THE KOBAL COLLECTION; 17b, Photo By EVERETT COLLECTION / REX FEATURES; 28m, Photo By FOTOS INTERNATIONAL / REX FEATURES; 28b, THE KOBAL COLLECTION / TOUCHSTONE/JERRY BRUCKHEIMER INC; 29t, HOLLYWOOD PICTURES / THE KOBAL COLLECTION; 29m, Photo By EVERETT COLLECTION / REX FEATURES; 29b, Photo By EVERETT COLLECTION / REX FEATURES; 30l, WARNER BROS / THE KOBAL COLLECTION; 30r, 20TH CENTURY FOX / THE KOBAL COLLECTION;

Every effort has been made to contact copyright holders of any material reproduced in this book. Any omissions will be rectified in subsequent printings if notice is given to the publishers.

An explanation of difficult words can be found in the glossary on page 31.

A CINEMATIC HISTORY OF ACTION & ADVENTURE

MARK WILSHIN

CONTENTS

INTRODUCTION

*Exploding with energy and excitement, the action movie is a spectacular extravaganza of high-speed car chases, big budget special effects and awe-inspiring stunts. With often only a single hero spoiling the plans of wicked villains, the action movie usually has a simple plot of good versus evil. While the action hero is often a **patriotic** American single-handedly defending moral values of truth and justice, the baddies are often foreign spies and criminals: Russian **communists**, French villains or **terrorists** and extremists. Breaking all the rules to bring baddies to justice, the hero is usually male, but more recent films have shown tough women fighting and shooting their way through equally punishing missions. With breathtaking fights, incredible explosions and fantastic editing, the action movie is pure entertainment, a visual wonderland to sit back and enjoy.*

EARLY ADVENTURERS

With handsome heroes, women in distress and evil villains, adventure movies of the silent era were a mix of exotic fantasy and daring heroics.

HEROES AND VILLAINS

While early adventure movies like *The Great Train Robbery* (1903) thrilled audiences with gunfights and horse-chases in the Wild West of the United States, *The Perils of Pauline* (1914) brought a different style to the adventure movie, as a brave hero rescues a beautiful and unlucky heroine from a wicked, scheming villain. Charting adventures in faraway lands, *The Prisoner of Zenda* (1922) is an early swashbuckling adventure as a man rescues his imprisoned royal cousin from an evil half-brother and the fortress of Zenda.

THE SQUAW MAN (1914)

Directed by Hollywood legend Cecil B. DeMille, The Squaw Man follows Captain Wynnegate, who has been accused of embezzling money, as he escapes from England to the United States. Out west, he meets and marries an Indian squaw. When Captain Wynnegate's old love Lady Diana arrives, he is in an awkward dilemma. The first feature-length film to be made in Hollywood, The Squaw Man was remade twice by DeMille himself.

THE GREAT TRAIN ROBBERY

ING "HOLD UP" OF THE "GOLD EXPRESS" BY FAMOUS WESTERN OUTLAWS

THE GREAT TRAIN ROBBERY (1903)

A landmark in cinema history, The Great Train Robbery was one of the first moving pictures to have a story. The tale of four bandits who hijack and rob a train, Edwin S. Porter's film revolutionized early cinema with location filming, new editing techniques, and special effects. Famous for its scene of a gangster firing directly into the camera, audiences were terrified, thinking they were really being shot at.

EXOTIC ADVENTURES

Using exotic locations to stir up adventure, silent movies like *Waxworks* (1924) and *Destiny* (1921) put several daring adventures into one film. In Fritz Lang's *Destiny*, a woman relives three stories of forbidden love in Persia, Venice, and China. The chariot races and sea battles of biblical times are recreated in *Ben Hur* (1925), while *Tarzan the Ape Man* (1932) explores the jungle for mystery and adventure, as a man raised by apes swings through the trees to rescue Jane and her father's expedition from a tribe of bloodthirsty dwarves.

THE THIEF OF BAGDAD (1924)

Set in the magical realms of Arabian Nights, The Thief of Bagdad *is a fantasy adventure of flying carpets, winged horses, sea monsters, and invisible cloaks. The first film to cost over one million U.S. dollars, the film uses trick photography and extravagant sets to portray the magic of the East.*

DOUGLAS FAIRBANKS

With his famous smile and athletic body, Douglas Fairbanks was Hollywood's first swashbuckling star. After starting on the stage, he fought his way on to the silver screen in comedies, before reaching super-stardom with adventure films like The Mask of Zorro *(1920),* The Three Musketeers *(1921), and* The Thief of Bagdad *(1924). He married the silent era star Mary Pickford and in 1919 they founded United Artists film studios with D.W. Griffith and Charlie Chaplin.*

SWASHBUCKLERS

Filled with spectacular swordfights, the swashbuckler movie was designed to show the star appeal of screen heroes like Douglas Fairbanks and Errol Flynn.

POPULAR PIRATES

Plundering ships on the high seas, pirate adventures became popular with *The Black Pirate* (1926), starring Douglas Fairbanks. Errol Flynn took over the role as the handsome swashbuckler in *Captain Blood* (1935) and *The Sea Hawk* (1940), robbing his way across the Caribbean and stealing women's hearts.

THE ADVENTURES OF ROBIN HOOD (1938)

Filmed in early Technicolor®, The Adventures of Robin Hood follows the legendary outlaw as he robs the rich and defends Saxons from the villainous Prince John. Winning archery competitions and fighting with Guy of Gisborne on castle staircases, Robin woos Maid Marion with his charm. With roaring fanfares and colourful pageantry, the film is a lavish mix of swashbuckling adventure and wit.

CUTTHROAT ISLAND (1995)

Armed with some sharp lines, Cutthroat Island follows the female captain of a pirate ship on a quest for hidden gold, as she tries to complete a treasure map.

PIRATES OF THE CARIBBEAN, CURSE OF THE BLACK PEARL (2003)

This film was inspired by the Disney theme park ride of the same name. It stars Johnny Depp as a pirate on a mission to win back the pirate ship 'The Black Pearl' and steal its stash of hidden treasure.

ERROL FLYNN

Born in Australia, Errol Flynn shot to stardom in Hollywood as the swashbuckling pirate in Captain Blood *(1935). Always the dashing hero, he was an outlaw in* The Adventures of Robin Hood *(1938) and a smooth-talking playboy in* The Adventures of Don Juan *(1948).*

CROSSED SWORDS

Set in a mythical past of brave heroes and spectacular swordfights, the silent film *Robin Hood* (1922) stars Douglas Fairbanks in a medieval extravaganza of lavish sets and costumes, which was later followed by Errol Flynn starring in *The Adventures of Robin Hood* (1938). Adapted from the novels by Alexandre Dumas, *The Three Musketeers* (1921) and *The Iron Mask* (1929) thrilled audiences with their intrigues and swashbuckling heroes. As the masked swordsman avenging Spanish injustice in California, Douglas Fairbanks played Zorro again in *Don Q Son of Zorro* (1925).

THE MARK OF ZORRO (1920)

Based on the novel <u>The Curse of Capistrano</u>, The Mark of Zorro *was Douglas Fairbanks' first swashbuckling role. While his quiet alter-ego Don Diego stays at home, the masked Zorro slides over rooftops, defending the downtrodden with his swordplay and agility.*

LURE OF THE SEA

Sailing the high seas in search of adventure and exotic islands, seafarers of the silver screen are faced with pirates as well as ruthless oceans.

MOBY DICK (1956)

Based on the classic novel by Herman Melville, Moby Dick stars Gregory Peck as Captain Ahab, leading the crew of the 'Pequod' on an expedition to find the whale that ripped his leg off. Depicting the battle against nature, John Huston's seafaring film shows Ahab's obsession with revenge on his enemy, Moby Dick.

NAVIGATING HISTORY

Recreating a time of exploration and discovery, seafaring films began with *The Sea Beast* (1926), a loose adaptation of <u>Moby Dick</u>. Starring Errol Flynn, Clark Gable, Marlon Brando and Mel Gibson as rebellious leader Fletcher Christian, *Mutiny on the Bounty* (1933, 1935, 1962 and 1984) has been filmed four times. It depicts the legendary mutiny of a ship's crew against the cruel Captain Bligh.

CAPTAINS COURAGEOUS (1937)

A coming-of-age tale, Captains Courageous follows the spoilt young son of a rich railway businessman, who is washed overboard from an ocean liner. Picked up by a Portuguese fishing boat, the boy works as one of the crew, slowly changing his ways as he adapts to the tough life of a fisherman at sea.

THE PERFECT STORM (2000)

Inspired by the true story of the fishing boat 'Andrea Gail', which was lost in a hurricane in October 1991, The Perfect Storm follows five fishermen trawling the oceans for a catch and ending up surrounded by enormous waves. The film depicts the human struggle against the forces of nature.

CAPTAIN HORATIO HORNBLOWER (1951)

Brimming with sea battles and swashbuckling adventures, this is the tale of a naval captain, fighting French and Spanish tall ships. Captain Horatio Hornblower was adapted from novels by C.S. Forester.

MASTER AND COMMANDER (2003)

Recreating life on board the British naval ship HMS Surprise, Master and Commander follows the ship's captain Lucky Jack, as he chases a larger and faster French ship around South American seas. The film accurately depicts furious battles and the ship's cramped conditions. It focuses on life on board the battleship, the friendship between the ship's captain and his surgeon, as well as the crew's short tempers and rising tensions.

DANGERS OF THE DEEP

Rather than the sea battles of the 18th century, modern sea adventures often focus on **Cold War** skirmishes in the Atlantic. In *The Abyss* (1989) divers attempt to rescue nuclear missiles from a sunken submarine, while *The Hunt for Red October* (1990) and *Crimson Tide* (1995) depict life on board a submarine, as tensions rise between the United States and Russia. The war between humans and creatures provides the story for films like *Jaws* (1975) and *Deep Blue Sea* (1999), where sharks terrorize the sea.

AGAINST THE ELEMENTS

Swimming through crocodile-infested waters and crossing treacherous ice peaks, the 'human versus nature' action movie often combines cruel landscapes with extreme sports. Struggling to survive in deserts, jungles and mountains, the daredevil hero provides audiences with serious thrills.

FLIGHT OF THE PHOENIX (1965)

After a plane crashes in the Sahara during a sandstorm, this film follows the passengers fighting heat, hunger, and each other as they try to construct a plane out of the wreckage.

THE AFRICAN QUEEN (1951)

This film stars Humphrey Bogart and Katharine Hepburn and follows a drunken riverboat captain and a sensible schoolteacher travelling downriver through the African jungle during World War I (1914–1918). Steering their way through crocodiles and rapids, the couple join the war by blowing up a German soldiers' boat. A classic mix of adventure, romance, and wartime heroics, the film focuses on the witty conversations between the strait-laced teacher and Bogart's Oscar Award-winning boatman.

WILD RIVERS

Extreme landscapes such as deserts and jungles are often the setting for cinematic stories of suffering and survival, but in river adventures like *Deliverance* (1972) holiday-makers become the victims of cruel locals in rural backwaters. In *The River Wild* (1994), a river rafting family has to combat both scheming criminals and the treacherous white waters.

ICY ADVENTURES

Set during the gold rush, *The Call of the Wild* (1935) also focuses on the human battle with nature in the wilds of Canada. The snow-capped mountain continues to combine dangerous landscapes with explosive action in films like *Vertical Limit* (2000) and *Cliffhanger* (1993), while other films focus on human survival. *Alive* (1993) follows a Uruguayan rugby team, who turn to **cannibalism** when their plane crashes in the mountains, while *Touching the Void* (2003) recreates the survival of a mountain climber, left for dead in the Andes.

VERTICAL LIMIT (2000)

Set on K2, the world's second highest mountain, Vertical Limit *depicts a young climber who comes face to face with nature at its most powerful, as he attempts to rescue his sister from an icy crevasse.*

WERNER HERZOG

*A leading director of the **German New Wave**, Werner Herzog often makes films about fanatical dreamers battling against nature. Filmed in the harsh Amazon jungle,* Aguirre, the Wrath of God *(1972) follows a Spanish explorer searching for El Dorado, the lost city of gold.* Fitzcarraldo *(1982) is centred round the foolishness of a rich rubber tycoon, hauling a steamship over a mountain to fulfil his dream of building an opera house in the jungle.*

Fitzcarraldo (1982)

JEREMIAH JOHNSON (1972)

Jeremiah Johnson *depicts a U.S. soldier who escapes the Mexican war to live as a mountain man, hunting furs in the Rocky Mountains. Taught the art of survival by an old fur-trapper, his simple life is interrupted by a feud with local indigenous Indians.*

DISASTER!

With **asteroids** heading for Earth, skyscrapers collapsing, and cities submerged beneath water, the disaster movie had its heyday in the 1970s. As glamorous partygoers scrabble to safety, the threat of impending doom brings out both the best and the worst in people.

ESCAPE!

Reducing buildings to ashes and streets to rubble, early disaster movies recreated historic catastrophes like the notorious 1906 earthquake in *San Francisco* (1936) and the great fire of 1871 in *In Old Chicago* (1937). The 1970s disaster movie opened with *The Poseidon Adventure* (1972), in which a tidal wave capsizes an ocean liner. *The Hindenburg* (1975) has a sabotaged airship exploding, while *Airport 1975* (1974) depicts a passenger jet flying without a pilot.

VOLCANO (1997)

With lava flowing down the streets of Los Angeles, Volcano *follows an earthquake expert and an emergency services controller rescuing people and their pets from explosions and fires, as magma surges up from the Earth's core.*

THE RAINS CAME (1939)

Set in colonial India, The Rains Came *depicts the love affair between an Indian doctor and a British Lady, as India is hit by a string of disasters, including earthquakes, floods, and the plague.*

ARMAGEDDON (1998)

The end of the world is near in Armageddon, *as an asteroid the size of Texas comes hurtling towards the Earth. Racing against time,* **NASA** *decides to send deep-core drillers into space, to plant a nuclear bomb inside the asteroid and blow it to pieces.*

ICEBERG AHOY!

Battling against natural disasters like earthquakes, tornadoes and volcanoes, movies like *Earthquake* (1974), *Twister* (1996), and *Dante's Peak* (1997) show the vulnerability of humans in the face of nature's power. *The Day After Tomorrow* (2004) examines human impact on the Earth, as **global warming** causes hurricanes, tidal waves, and floods. With asteroids racing towards the Earth, sci-fi disaster films focus on the end of the world, in films like *Deep Impact* (1998), which shows society in chaos as only a million people are selected to survive. Director James Cameron's disaster epic *Titanic* (1997) shows the vanity of humans, as an 'unsinkable' ship hits an iceberg.

THE CORE (2003)

With San Francisco's Golden Gate Bridge melting and the Colosseum in Rome reduced to rubble, The Core *depicts a world in peril, as scientists discover the Earth's core has stopped turning. Travelling to the centre of the Earth, a group of 'terranauts' have to jump-start the core with nuclear bombs.*

THE TOWERING INFERNO (1974)

Featuring an all-star cast, The Towering Inferno *is set in the fictional Glass Tower, the world's tallest skyscraper. Celebrating the opening of the tower at a party on the top floor, the architect and San Francisco's high society are trapped, when faulty wiring sparks a fire. Inspired by the construction of the World Trade Center in the early 1970s,* The Towering Inferno *plays with the audience's fear of a skyscraper catching fire. The action keeps us terrified as party guests try to escape to a neighbouring tower.*

TREASURE QUEST

Risking snake pits, booby traps and barbaric tribes, treasure hunting adventures began with the cliffhanging serials of the 1930s and 1940s. Featuring jaw-dropping stunts and spectacular special effects, the treasure quest combines clever humour with thrills and suspense.

TREASURE HUNTERS

With heroines tied up to railway tracks and heroes dangling from cliffs, early adventure serials like *Spy Smasher* (1942) inspired Indiana Jones' treasure quests. Dodging boulders and outrunning **Nazis** in *Raiders of the Lost Ark* (1981), Jones is cinema's ultimate treasure hunter.

TREASURE OF THE SIERRA MADRE (1948)

Directed by John Huston, The Treasure of the Sierra Madre *follows three drifters who head to the Mexican hills in the search for gold. As greed, paranoia, and suspicion take over, the three friends turn against each other and their dreams of gold turn to dust.*

TREASURE ISLAND (1950)

Adapted from the novel by Robert Louis Stevenson, Treasure Island *follows a young boy who braves the high seas, pirates, and the treacherous Long John Silver, to find buried treasure on a Caribbean island.*

INDIANA JONES AND THE LAST CRUSADE (1989)

Steven Spielberg's favourite film of the trilogy, Indiana Jones and the Last Crusade *follows the whip-cracking adventurer across Europe in search of his kidnapped father and the Holy Grail. Racing against the Nazis to find the cup of eternal life, Indiana Jones and his father brave rat-infested crypts, booby-trapped temples and a Zeppelin airship in Berlin. Full of witty one-liners and thrilling chase sequences, the film recaptures the adventure and excitement of* Raiders of the Lost Ark (1981), *after the less successful* Indiana Jones and the Temple of Doom *(1984).*

PERILOUS JOURNEYS

Romancing the Stone (1984) combines adventure with humour, with a novelist dodging bullets in the jungle to rescue her kidnapped sister and find a rare diamond. More recent films like *The Mummy* (1999) have updated the treasure quest with supernatural monsters, while *National Treasure* (2004) uses clues to uncover a treasure hidden by the Founding Fathers of the United States.

LARA CROFT: TOMB RAIDER (2001)

Wielding shotguns and pistols, Lara Croft: Tomb Raider is a video game adaptation, which follows heroine Lara Croft as she searches mystical temples for the magical clock of ages.

STEVEN SPIELBERG

One of Hollywood's most successful directors, Spielberg shot to stardom with his action horror movie Jaws *(1975) before making the adventure-packed Indiana Jones series. From sci-fi to war epics, Steven Spielberg's films appeal to many people, with crime capers like* Catch Me If You Can *(2002) and Martian invasions in* War of the Worlds *(2005).*

BOND, JAMES BOND

Equipped with hi-tech gadgets, this handsome and sophisticated spy fights with iron-fisted villains and irresistible Bond girls all over the world. Shaken but not stirred, 007 continues to amuse and thrill audiences with clever wisecracks and daredevil escapades in these playful spy adventures.

LICENCE TO KILL

Carrying a bullet-deflecting watch, an electronic safecracker and a cigarette gun, James Bond is cinema's ultimate secret agent. Inspired by Ian Fleming's novels, the James Bond film series started with *Dr No* (1962), in which 007 travels to Jamaica to defeat a doctor with a mad plan for world domination. Fighting **Cold War** villains from Russia and the organized crime ring SPECTRE, Bond has saved the world from nuclear missiles and **atom bombs**. In *Thunderball* (1965) he fights with enemy agents on the ocean floor, while in *You Only Live Twice* (1967) he battles with his arch-enemy, Blofeld, in a rocket station hidden inside a volcano.

IAN FLEMING

Inspired by his experiences as an intelligence officer during World War II, Ian Fleming wrote twelve novels and nine short stories about the smooth-talking spy James Bond. Casino Royale was first published in 1953. Fleming wrote all his novels from his Jamaican beach house, Goldeneye.

FROM RUSSIA WITH LOVE (1963)

The second film in the James Bond series, From Russia with Love sees 007 lured into a sinister trap by criminal organization SPECTRE in revenge for the killing of their leader Dr No. Armed with an explosive briefcase and a sniper rifle, the gentleman spy outwits ruthless assassins and Russian spies in Istanbul, and on board the Orient Express.

MOONRAKER (1979)

Following the sci-fi craze of the 1970s, 007 was launched into space in Moonraker to fight an evil millionaire's plan to start a master race in outer space. More light-hearted than some other Bond films, Moonraker features the iron-toothed killer Jaws.

A MAN WITH A GUN

Played by Sean Connery, George Lazenby, Roger Moore, Timothy Dalton, and Pierce Brosnan, 007 has starred in twenty films from *Dr No* (1962) to *Die Another Day* (2002). Seducing women and toppling villains, the famous spy continues to thrill audiences with explosive adventures in exotic locations.

OCTOPUSSY (1983)

Braving crocodile-infested waters, mad Russian generals, and nuclear bombs, Octopussy sees James Bond investigate the death of 009 and the porcelain egg he dies clutching.

GOLDFINGER (1964)

Arguably the ultimate bond movie, Goldfinger follows 007 as he trails the rich businessman and smuggler Goldfinger, who is plotting to destroy gold bullion at Fort Knox. Driving an Aston Martin car, complete with machine guns, Bond wrangles with lethal laser beams and with Oddjob, a baddie with a razor sharp bowler hat.

GOLDEN EYE (1995)

Bringing Bond into the 1990s, Golden Eye follows the villainous plot of a criminal gang to fire a nuclear satellite into London. Armed with a pen-grenade and a machine gun, Bond shoots his way through Russia's criminals.

SPIES LIKE US

Bristling with **Cold War** *paranoia, the spy thriller depicts deadly double agents making their way across Europe with style and stealth. Often more realistic, the spy flick goes one better than Bond, with endless trickery, suspicion and double-crossing.*

ESPIONAGE

Inspired by the real-life secret agent, *Mata Hari* (1931) follows Germany's glamorous spy during World War I, as she seduces Russian officers and swipes secret documents in Paris. While *Confessions of a Nazi Spy* (1939) is centred round Nazi agents in the United States before World War II (1939–1945), the spy thriller really peaked during the Cold War with films like *The Spy Who Came in from the Cold* (1965), where a British spy crosses into East Germany to spread misleading information.

SPIONE (1928)

With stolen secret documents, murdered diplomats, and enemy spies, Spione *defines the rules of the spy adventure, as special agent 326 foils a spy ring led by a wheelchair-bound master criminal dreaming of world domination.*

THE IPCRESS FILE (1968)

This film follows an underpaid spy in glasses and raincoat, as he battles to track the spy behind the kidnapping and brainwashing of British scientists.

WHERE EAGLES DARE (1968)

With a mission to rescue an American general from behind enemy lines during World War II, Where Eagles Dare *is a web of intrigue and double-crossing, as special agents fight on cable-cars to make their way into the 'lion's den'.*

DOUBLE DEALING

With business conspiracies and double-crossing agents, the modern spy adventure is a hair-raising mix of treachery and deception. In *Spy Game* (2001) a CIA agent must outwit his colleagues as he rescues the spy he trained from a Chinese prison, while *The Bourne Identity* (2002) combines stylish visuals with fast car chases, as a trained assassin recovers his lost identity.

RONIN (1982)

Meaning 'a Samurai warrior without a master', Ronin follows a group of criminal experts planning to steal a valuable briefcase. With stunning car chase sequences, Ronin is a clever thriller of mind games and betrayal.

JOHN LE CARRÉ

After working for the British Foreign Service, David Cornwell became a novelist, under the pen name John le Carré. Writing novels, like <u>The Spy Who Came in from the Cold</u>, *he writes about secret agents in Eastern Europe.*

MISSION: IMPOSSIBLE (1995)

Inspired by the 1960s U.S. television series, Mission: Impossible *stars Tom Cruise as Ethan Hunt, a special agent on a mission, which goes horribly wrong when the rest of his team is killed. Suspected of being a mole, Hunt has to dodge bullets until he can clear his name and find the real baddie. With plenty of plot twists,* Mission: Impossible *is a slick action thriller with exciting chases and hi-tech heists.*

CONSPIRACY

Inspired by real-life political intrigues, such as President Kennedy's assassination, the 1970s saw a rise in conspiracy thrillers in which ordinary people are caught in political scheming and government corruption.

NORTH BY NORTHWEST (1959)

Named after a compass direction that does not exist, North by Northwest follows advertising executive Roger Thornhill as he travels across America, after being mistaken for a secret agent and framed for murder. Thornhill is drawn into a deadly spy game, as he tries to stay one step ahead. With famous sequences of a crop-dusting plane attacking Cary Grant in a cornfield and a shoot-out on Mount Rushmore, this film was the last of Hitchcock's notorious man-on-the-run thrillers.

ENEMY OF THE STATE (1998)

Using spy cameras and traced calls, this film examines government surveillance, as the National Security Agency uses spy satellites to track a lawyer with incriminating evidence against them.

THE MANCHURIAN CANDIDATE (1962)

*A **Cold War** conspiracy thriller, The Manchurian Candidate follows a U.S. officer, who was brainwashed by **Communists** during the Korean War. Hypnotized when he sees the Queen of Hearts, the secret assassin is controlled by his scheming mother.*

POLITICAL PLOTS

Full of the paranoia of the 1970s, *The Conversation* (1974) depicts a surveillance expert trapped in a deadly plot of corporate espionage and murder, while *The Parallax View* (1974) uncovers the chilling conspiracy behind the murder of a senator and seven witnesses. The Watergate scandal is also explored in *All the President's Men* (1976), as two journalists discover a trail of crimes and cover-ups leading all the way to the United States' White House.

THE PELICAN BRIEF (1993)

Famous for his government conspiracy novels, John Grisham's The Pelican Brief, *is a thriller about a law student and a newspaper reporter who team up to uncover a corporate conspiracy. Avoiding hit-men and hired heavies, they discover a trail leading all the way to the President of the United States.*

MIND GAMES

Many modern political thrillers, like *The Firm* (1993) and *Conspiracy Theory* (1997), depict normal people involved in sinister schemes. In *In the Line of Fire* (1993) a secret service agent is full of guilt because he could not prevent Kennedy's assassination. He becomes involved in a deadly game with a man determined to kill the new president.

TOM CLANCY

Tom Clancy has become a best-selling author. Some of his political thrillers have been made into movies, such as The Hunt for Red October *(1990)*, Patriot Games *(1992)*, Clear and Present Danger *(1994)*, and The Sum of all Fears *(2002)*, in which his famous CIA agent hero, Jack Ryan, saves the world from nuclear war and terrorism.*

Harrison Ford in *Patriot Games* (1992)

EAST MEETS WEST

While Hong Kong action cinema has long amazed audiences with high-kicks, karate and wire-assisted kung-fu, Hollywood has recently borrowed from Eastern martial arts movies to create its own spectacular fights.

KUNG-FU FIGHTING

Famous for its martial arts movies, Hong Kong cinema had its heyday in the 1970s with director Bruce Lee's action flicks, *Fists of Fury* (1971) and *Way of the Dragon* (1972). After Lee's death, kung-fu fighting was updated in films like *A Better Tomorrow* (1986) and *The Killer* (1989).

RUSH HOUR (1998)

A martial arts comedy, Rush Hour *follows a police inspector from Hong Kong and a loudmouthed LA cop, hunting for a Chinese diplomat's kidnapped daughter. With its clever one-liners, Rush Hour makes light of the culture clash between East and West.*

ENTER THE DRAGON (1973)

The definitive martial arts movie, Enter the Dragon stars kung-fu master Bruce Lee, as he investigates the activities of criminal king Han, who holds a martial arts tournament to cover up his illegal drug dealings. Discovering Han is also responsible for his sister's death, Lee decides to wreak revenge on him. A combination of amazing stunts and Eastern spirituality, the film climaxes with a hall of mirrors showdown between Lee and Han. A Chinese American co-production, the film was intended to introduce Lee to American audiences, but tragically he died a few weeks before the film's première.

MORE MARTIAL ARTS

As many Hong Kong actors and directors went to the United States in search of bigger budgets, Eastern martial arts have blended with Western action movies, in films like *Shanghai Noon* (2000). With the success of films like *Crouching Tiger Hidden Dragon* (2000), Hollywood has used the traditions of kung-fu in *The Matrix* (1999) and swordfights in *Kill Bill* (2003).

ROMEO MUST DIE (2000)

Updating Shakespeare's Romeo and Juliet, *this film depicts an ex-cop, who breaks out of prison to avenge the death of his brother, but gets caught in a war between the Chinese mafia and the African-American mob.*

BULLETPROOF MONK (2003)

Based on a comic strip, Bulletproof Monk *stars Chow Yun Fat as a kung-fu fighting monk and protector of a holy scroll, who recruits an American pickpocket as his replacement.*

WARRIORS OF HEAVEN AND EARTH (2004)

An epic swashbuckling adventure, Warriors of Heaven and Earth *follows an Imperial officer on the trail of a soldier in the Gobi desert. When a group of monks carrying a precious cargo comes under attack from bandits, the two sparring swordsmen unite to protect them.*

JOHN WOO

Directing martial arts movies in Hong Kong, John Woo created breathtaking 'gun-fu' thrillers with intricately choreographed fight scenes and gun-toting anti-heroes. Ultra-violent and realistic, Woo's Hong Kong movies A Better Tomorrow *(1986) and* The Killer *(1989) became favourites, while his Hollywood blockbusters* Hard Target *(1993) and* Broken Arrow *(1996) suffered under studio interference.*

CLIFFHANGER (1993)

Starring Sylvester Stallone as a mountain rescue climber, Cliffhanger features a 40 foot jump across a mountain crevasse and a fight on top of a helicopter, as Stallone tries to outwit a band of thieves.

LETHAL WEAPON (1987)

This is an action-packed cop movie, starring Mel Gibson and Danny Glover as two mismatched cops on the trail of Los Angeles' most powerful and violent drug ring. Surviving shootouts, car chases, and explosions, the two cops gradually learn to get along.

TOUGH GUYS

The big stars of box-office blockbusters, Sylvester Stallone, Arnold Schwarzenegger and Bruce Willis, are tough guys who play by their own rules, fighting villains, protecting the innocent, and saving the world from destruction through sheer strength and determination.

DIE HARD 2 (1990)

With Bruce Willis as cop John McClane, Die Hard 2 takes place one year after the hostage-taking of Die Hard (1988). Waiting for his wife at Dulles International airport, McClane learns of a plot by a terrorist group to take over the airport control tower. With dozens of planes circling the skies, waiting to land, McClane has to regain control of air communications before planes start running out of fuel and fall from the sky. Thrilling audiences with shootouts and explosions, the film climaxes with a fight on the wing of a moving plane.

LAW OF THE JUNGLE

With vigilante cops and soldiers seeking rough justice, action cinema often focuses on heroes on the wrong side of the law. In *Mad Max* (1979), Mel Gibson plays an ex-police officer seeking revenge for the brutal murder of his wife and son, while Sylvester Stallone's *Rambo* (1982) sees a highly trained soldier clash with a small town sheriff.

ESCAPE FROM ALCATRAZ (1979)

Based on a true story, Escape from Alcatraz *is a low-key escape thriller, starring Clint Eastwood as one of three prisoners who escapes from the high-security island prison in San Francisco bay by sailing away on a raft made of raincoats.*

HARD COPS

Making his name as a tough cop in *Dirty Harry* (1971), Clint Eastwood started a tradition of rule-breaking policemen. In *Die Hard* (1988), Bruce Willis is a lone detective armed only with a pistol, caught in a cat-and-mouse game with ruthless robbers.

ARNOLD SCHWARZENEGGER

Born in Austria, Arnold Schwarzenegger moved to the United States aged 21, where he became a famous bodybuilder. Schwarzenegger used his physique to break into acting, with films like Conan the Barbarian *(1982). Normally playing tough action heroes, Schwarzenegger is still most famous for his role in* The Terminator *(1984).*

INVINCIBLE

Bullet-proof warriors were the heroes of many action films in the 1980s and 1990s, defeating villains with powerful guns and big muscles. Jean Claude van Damme, the 'muscles from Brussels', made his name in *Universal Soldier* (1992) while Steven Seagal starred in the action thriller *Under Siege* (1992). Schwarzenegger is perhaps the most popular muscleman, as a soldier in *Predator* (1987) and the gun-wielding 'Terminator'.

TO THE EDGE AND BACK

Trains, planes, and automobiles are often used in action thrillers for hair-raising stunts and death-defying battles. Racing at breakneck speed against rivals, villains, and ticking bombs, the fast-paced action movie excites audiences with fast races and hot cars.

CON AIR (1997)

Featuring an all-star cast, Con Air follows the skyjacking of a prison plane by a gang of murderers and criminals, as one man on his way home tries to stop them. With a plane landing in the middle of Las Vegas, Con Air is full of spectacular explosions and suspense.

JERRY BRUCKHEIMER

Bruckheimer is famous for producing films with adrenaline-pumping action sequences. He is the Hollywood producer behind films from Flashdance *(1983) to* National Treasure *(2004). With simple plots and elaborate special effects, Bruckheimer's films are fast and furious, such as* Top Gun *(1986). He has produced many modern blockbusters, from the action comedy* Pirates of the Caribbean *(2003) to* King Arthur *(2004).*

AIR ACTION

After early flying adventures like *The Spirit of St Louis* (1957), modern action movies have entertained audiences with high-tech planes and jets. In *Top Gun* (1986) Tom Cruise plays a gifted pilot, battling against other fighter pilots in the skies for the title of 'top gun'. Extreme sports also have audiences on the edge of their seats as skydiving bank robbers are chased through the air by Keanu Reeves in *Point Break* (1991).

THE ROCK (1996)

When an army general takes revenge on the United States government by stealing weapons and hijacking the prison island of Alcatraz, an escaped prisoner and a chemical weapons expert work together to save the hostages and stop the bombs.

TOP SPEED

Set in the world of extreme sports, *xXx* (2002) updates the James Bond spy adventure, with a criminal thrill-seeker turned spy chasing Russian criminals on motorbikes and snowboards. In *Days of Thunder* (1990) and *The Fast and the Furious* (2001), car racing provides hair-raising thrills, while *Speed* (1994) depicts a cat-and-mouse game between a crazed bomber and a rookie cop, as he tries to free hostages on a bus speeding towards an explosive end.

THE FAST AND THE FURIOUS (2001)

Set in Los Angeles, The Fast and the Furious *examines the underground culture of street racing with Vin Diesel as a gang leader, who organizes high-speed motorway chases. The film features breakneck races and spectacular stunts.*

THE WAGES OF FEAR (1953)

Set in the South American jungle, The Wages of Fear *follows four men stranded in a small village suffering intense heat, poverty, and unemployment. When an American oil company offers them $2,000 each to transport highly explosive nitro-glycerine through the jungle, the four men seize the opportunity, risking their lives to cross bridges and lakes in this gripping journey of suspense. Directed by Henri-Georges Clouzot, nicknamed the French Hitchcock,* The Wages of Fear *puts humans to the test, in this feat of endurance.*

FILM TECHNOLOGY

STUNTS

Hanging off cliffs, leaping across speeding trains and falling from skyscrapers, breathtaking stunts are essential to action movies. Performed by professional stunt doubles, adrenaline-pumping stunts are planned with enormous care.

FALLING OFF BUILDINGS

While stuntmen traditionally jumped off buildings on to huge airbags on the ground to break their fall, many falls are now performed using a fan descender. Attached by a harness to a length of wire, the stunt double falls with greater control, as the speed of the uncoiling wire is controlled by a slow fan.

PLAYING WITH FIRE

Fire stunts are highly dangerous and require careful planning. Using fuels that burn brightly at low temperatures, the stunt double wears a fire-resistant bodysuit and mask to enable him to withstand flames for up to 30 seconds, while polymer gels are also used to make ordinary clothes flameproof.

TRASHING THE CAR

Hugely popular in action movies, car stunts require specialized training and must be intricately planned and choreographed. In car chases, a concealed ramp is often used to flip speeding cars over, while air rams are combined with explosions for highly charged car crashes. With air cannons fitted into the boot of a car, a ram is launched by a blast of compressed air, which tips the car over. This is usually combined with a controlled explosion to mask the air ram and make the effect even more spectacular.

GLOSSARY

asteroids
small rocky planets travelling round the Sun

atom bomb
bomb whose explosive power comes from the smallest part of a chemical element that can possibly exist, an atom

cannibal
person who eats the flesh of other human beings

Cold War
state of hostility between nations without an actual war. The term usually describes the situation between the Soviet Union and the United States between 1945 and 1991.

communism
political theory that social class should be abolished and all land and wealth that a country has should be shared out equally

German New Wave
movement in German cinema of the 1960s and 1970s, led by a group of experimental filmmakers

global warming
gradual increase in the overall temperature of the Earth's atmosphere due to increased levels of carbon dioxide and other pollutants

NASA
National Aeronautics and Space Administration (based in the U.S.)

Nazi
member of the National Socialist German Worker's party

nuclear
using energy released in the reaction of atomic nuclei

patriotism
term that describes love or devotion to your country

terrorist
person who uses violence and intimidation in an attempt to achieve political aims

INDEX